Old KIRKBY LONSDALE
And the Rainbow Parish
by
Michael J. Hall

This book has been published to mark the 30th anniversary of the Kirkby Lonsdale & District Civic Society, and was put together with the invaluable help and support of members of the society.

Looking downstream towards Devil's Bridge in the late 1940s, with the new Stanley Bridge visible through the central arch.

© Michael J. Hall 2004
First published in the United Kingdom, 2004,
by Stenlake Publishing Ltd.
Telephone: 01290 551122
Printed by Cordfall Ltd., Glasgow, G21 2QA

ISBN 1 84033 306 5

The publishers regret that they cannot supply copies of any pictures featured in this book.

A procession passing in front of the Royal Hotel in Market Square to celebrate the Coronation of King Edward VII on 8 August 1902.

ACKNOWLEDGEMENTS

The Civic Society would like to extend its most grateful thanks to everyone who has made this venture possible. In particular those who have loaned their precious photographs and given permission to use them, namely: Ruth Carling, Joan Fishwick, Jean German, George Harrison, Kath Hayhurst, Graham Mathews, Audrey Phillips, Ian Radford, James Thompson, Harry Willan, and William Wilson. We would also like to thank the Stanley Robinson Archive at Casterton School, the Westmorland Gazette, the Local Studies section of Kendal Library for permission to reproduce the picture on page 48, www.Aerofilms.com of Potters Bar for the picture on page 4, and www.francisfrith.co.uk for the lower picture on page 7. The author would like to extend special thanks to George Harrison, Audrey Phillips, Peter Spillard, William Wilson and Michael Harrison who read the initial draft and made valuable suggestions for its improvement.

FURTHER READING

The books listed below were used by the author during his research. None of them are available from Stenlake Publishing. Those interested in finding out more are advised to contact their local bookshop or reference library.

The Annals of Kirkby Lonsdale and Lunesdale Today,
   A. Pearson, D. Kyle, A. Phillips, M. Gresson, 1996
The Doings of a Country Solicitor, A. Pearson, 1947
A Stroll through Kirkby Lonsdale, Mary Gresson, 1996
Kirkby Lonsdale and District in Times Past, Elizabeth Breay,
   Audrey Cox, Norah Hutton, Dennis Dixon, 1985
Britain in Old Photographs – Kirkby Lonsdale & District,
   Nigel and Phillip Dalziel, 1996
My Valley: The Life and Times of Jonty Wilson, Kirkby Lonsdale Blacksmith, T. Wilson-Goad, 1993
A History of Mansergh and Rigmaden, the People and their Farms, Olive Wilson, 1991 (unpublished but available in Kendal Library)
The Story of Lupton, 1301–1956, Frances Mason
From Source to Sea – A Brief History of the Lune Valley, Peter R. Williamson, 2001

INTRODUCTION

Artefacts dating back to the late Stone Age show that the central Lune Valley has been inhabited for several thousand years. In their turn waves of immigrants including Romans, Normans and Anglo–Saxons traversed the valley, settling and interbreeding with the local people. With the resultant growth of population, river crossings became strategically more important. One of these, situated on the River Lune almost at its midpoint between source and sea, was to become the site of Kirkby Lonsdale.

The town stands on a commanding bluff near a sweeping curve of the river close to a fordable crossing point, a site that could command military, packhorse and drove routes to the north and south as well as a passage towards the west coast from inland. Another feature that has shaped the character of Kirkby Lonsdale is the presence of rocky limestone promontories on the river bank strong enough to allow the construction of Devil's Bridge. This ancient monument is one of the finest river spans in the North West and has withstood flood and tempest for over 700 years. Research by local historian David Smail suggests that the original structure dates back to 1294. Two hundred years earlier, a Saxon church close to the site of St Mary's was given by Ivo de Taillebois, Baron of Kendal, to the Abbey of St Mary's in York. The church, under the patronage of Trinity College, Cambridge, is now in the Diocese of Carlisle but has retained strong links with York.

In the Tudor period (1485–1603) the documented history of the district becomes more abundant and landmarks still familiar today – such as Abbot Hall, Killington Hall and Middleton Hall – begin to appear in the records. Events such as an outbreak of plague in Mansergh in 1578 in which nineteen people died are recorded, and the names of families destined to shape the social history and land distribution of the district begin to appear. These include those of Carus, Conder, Curwen, Shuttleworth, and the Wilsons of Underley.

During the Stuart and Victorian periods (1603–1901) St Mary's Church was thoroughly restored and the building of the earliest small chapels such as those at Middleton, Mansergh, and Hutton Roof took place. Local turnpike roads were opened and tollbars set up at Casterton, Ireby and elsewhere. The first issue of the *Westmorland Gazette* appeared on 23 May 1818. More familiar family names appear, such as the Paget-Tomlinsons, Cavendish-Bentincks and the Wilsons of Rigmaden. In addition to these, the names of less exalted families upon which the day-to-day life of the district so much depended also begin to be noted.

From the nineteenth century onwards building proceeded apace. Many landmarks, such as the workhouse (1811), old Lunefield (1816), the New Market Place (1822), the Clergy Daughters' School (1823), Underley Hall (1825), Rigmaden and Mansergh Church (1827), Casterton Church (1833), Barbon Manor (1863) and The Biggins (1895) were built during the 1800s. In 1840 Queen Adelaide stayed at the Rose and Crown, after which it became the Royal Hotel. William Sturgeon gave his famous lectures on electricity and optics at the Green Dragon Inn in 1847, and the Kirkby Lonsdale Gas Company was established in 1850.

Prior to 1850 Kirkby's ancient history can only be viewed through its remaining monuments, the few paintings and etchings that exist, and in the mind's eye of the imagination. However, in 1839 the daguerreotype process of photography was first publicly described, and by the 1840s the process had evolved sufficiently to gain widespread use. The age of photography had arrived and with it the ability to capture the present as it really was. Photographic images add greatly to the written records, and conjure up vivid pictures of those early days. Such images have the ability to connect the present with the past and provide a strong sense of place, especially for those many families who can trace their ancestry back over generations. For newcomers, being able to build a picture of the town's past is also a valuable asset.

This book of old and not-so-old photographs mainly consists of images of Kirkby Lonsdale and district taken between the late nineteenth and mid-twentieth centuries. It covers what is known locally as the 'Rainbow Parish' of Kirkby Lonsdale, which includes Barbon, Casterton, Hutton Roof, Lupton, Mansergh and Middleton. Though many of the pictures are of familiar scenes, the great majority have not been published before. The book's assembly began in 2002 to mark the thirtieth anniversary of the founding of the Kirkby Lonsdale & District Civic Society, an organisation whose objective is to strive to preserve all that is best in our area. It is hoped that future generations may look back with pleasure at our efforts once today has faded into yesterday.

Kirkby Lonsdale has filled out considerably since this aerial photograph was taken in the mid-1950s. The row of houses at the lower right is Harling Bank. Construction commenced in the 1930s with a partnership between Percy Harrison (wine merchant), Herbert Dean (grocer) and one William Clear of London who was the landlord of a pub called the Red Lion in Tottenham. However, the venture was not very successful and the road was not completed until after the Second World War. Above Harling Bank are fields (including Smithy Field, which lay behind Jonty Wilson's smithy) which are now occupied by Fairgarth and Fairgarth Drive. Also visible is the former National School at the lower left, St Mary's Church, the Gazebo, Church Brow Cottage, Market Square, the gas holder adjacent to the Island, the bowling club and the two bridges over the River Lune.

St Mary's Church tower provides a commanding view of the town and River Lune. This view from the 1960s looks south and shows the wrought iron gates at the end of the Church Street entrance to the churchyard. These were constructed by William Jackson in 1823 in a beer house in Tunstall that doubled as a blacksmiths. They cost £39 5s 10¾d, plus 4s for paint and 6d for oil. The wrought iron gates at the Queen's Square entrance were made by William's brother John a few years later. Both sets remain fully functional today. The open fields in the distance are now the site of the former police houses and car parks.

The Norman doorway of St Mary's Church being opened by the verger some time before the First World War. Though now very weathered, the arch originally carried two dragons on the left-hand side. The pillar shafts and oak door were renewed as part of restoration work carried out in 1866.

St Mary's Church, visible in the aerial view on page 4, was extensively restored by the Earl of Bective in 1866 when the roof line was raised, battlements added, stonework renovated and the old south porch (dating from the mid-1500s) replaced. Fortunately, the redundant porch was not destroyed but re-erected as a summer house in the garden adjacent to Green Close. It is now a Grade II listed building in its own right, and its description states that it has a 'slate roof, gable with kneelers, moulded segmental entrance arch with keystone, moulded jambs and impost band with shallow rustications'.

Now planted with flowers, the horse trough in Queen's Square carries the inscription: 'Erected by public subscription gratefully to record the restoration of the Parish Church of Kirkby Lonsdale by Lord Kenlis. AD 1868' (Lord Kenlis was the Earl of Bective). On the reverse of this picture are the words 'Picnic in Kirkby Lonsdale, 22 May 1920'. Clearly this outing was an all-male affair!

The view looking north along Main Street from Market Square, reproduced from a postcard sent on 12 February 1904. The shop on the left beyond the Royal Hotel carries the wording 'Watchmaker – Pailthorp' and traded under that name for over 100 years, finally changing hands in 2002. The premises on the right is still a chemist to this day but is no longer Bayliff's. After Queen Adelaide (widow of King William IV) stayed there for one night on 23 July 1840, the Rose and Crown was renamed the Royal Hotel. The iron railings outside the chemist and the Royal were removed during the Second World War as part of the war effort.

Looking south along Main Street towards Town End in 1899. At the time the road was still cobbled, the shop behind the lamp post was trading as 'D. Bowers Boot and Clog maker' and the lamp stood where the Monument would be erected in 1905. Below the window of the cobblers are sloping doors – now replaced by stonework – that gave access to the cellar. Visible on the facade of both the Royal and the Waverley Temperance Hotel is the CTC emblem of the Cyclists' Touring Club. The presence of these two hotels, not to mention the Green Dragon Inn (now the Snooty Fox), attest to the fact that even then Kirkby Lonsdale was a centre for visitors.

Market Square decorated for the celebration of Queen Victoria's Diamond Jubilee on 20 June 1897. A procession led by the coach of the High Sheriff, Dr W. S. Paget-Tomlinson, can be seen approaching down New Road. Also present was the Kirkby Lonsdale Brass Band conducted by William Taylforth, and a company of the 2nd (Westmorland) Volunteer Battalion of the Border Regiment. The lamp post in front of the Royal Hotel was removed to the rear of the square when the Monument (page 12) was built in 1905, and still stands there today. To the left of the Royal are the premises of Brierley, carpenters of Barbon. That building now has a third storey, added by Alfred Harris who formerly lived at Lunefield (page 36). This may be one of a series of photographs taken by Robert L. Simpson, who lived at Ivy Cottage near to what is now Jingling Lane.

Another business whose function has remained unchanged for over a century is the sweet shop in Market Square, seen here in 1902/03. The doors under the window have been removed since its day as a cobblers (page 7, lower) and replaced by stonework. Various suggestions have been made as to the identity of the person in the doorway, who may be a member of the Willan, Thornborrow or Remington families.

The market square is in many ways the hub of towns such as Kirkby Lonsdale. Strictly speaking this is the New Market Square as it only opened for trading in 1822, having been created out of the gardens of Jackson's Hall (now the Royal Hotel). Prior to that, markets were held on land between the Sun Inn and the junction of Main Street and Market Street, and in nearby Swine and Horse Markets off Mill Brow. This image, taken before the construction of the Monument in 1905, shows the square fulfilling its most traditional function, that of a cattle market. The sheep pens and swings on the right would have been erected for the duration of the market.

Market Square photographed from the upper floor of the Royal Hotel, probably in the 1950s, by which time the upper ribs of the Monument had been removed. The building in the background with the curved gable carries the date 1914 and was built by Sir Henry Cavendish-Bentinck as a Conservative Club. Carling's market stall is in the foreground.

This postcard was published to mark the official dedication of the Monument on Saturday 25 February 1905. Designed by architects Paley & Austin of Lancaster, it was given to Kirkby Lonsdale by the Revd Llewellyn-Davies (marked with two crosses and standing against the right-hand buttress) in memory of his wife. Seated to his right are Dr W. S. Paget-Tomlinson, J. R. Pickard (centre) and the solicitor Alec Pearson. The man standing at the extreme left is the curate, Bertie Williams; to his left are J. Kassell, clerk to the council (wearing a white carnation), William Taylforth and Dr Wylie GP. The group on the right includes Billy Wolfenden (gents' outfitter and haberdasher), John Taylforth (schoolmaster), and John Wilman (proprietor of the Royal Hotel). The eight upper ogee ribs that supported the central cross were removed in the late 1940s, by which time they had become weakened by traffic vibration and the poor quality of stone used.

A visiting fair was always a highlight, especially for the town's youngsters. In this picture, taken in 1905 soon after the dedication of the Monument, a Whitsuntide Market is accompanied by a ride called the 'Flying Cockerels'.

The death of King Edward VII on 6 May 1910 was marked in towns and villages up and down Britain. This picture shows the memorial procession which took place in Kirkby Lonsdale on 20 May 1910. Leading the parade is the Kirkby Lonsdale Brass Band followed by a half-company of volunteers of the Border Regiment. The picture, looking down Main Street, was taken from the room in which George Harrison was born. To the left is J. Irving Richardson's shop and to the right the Dean family's grocers.

Before the widespread introduction of radio and television, public proclamations were an important method of communicating national news. This image shows Market Square being used for a royal proclamation on the evening of Wednesday 11 May 1910 announcing the accession to the throne of King George V. The occasion was attended by the High Sheriff, John Rankin, and began with a procession from the council offices. At its head, a council workman carried the Union flag. Also taking part was a local detachment of the Territorials under Captain F. Pearson; the Cadet Corps under Sergeant W. E. Fishwick; and groups of pupils from the elementary and grammar schools marshalled by John Taylforth. On the platform are High Sheriff John Rankin; the Right Honourable Lord Henry Cavendish-Bentinck; Dr T. G. Mathews (medical officer); William Taylforth (council chairman); L. C. Kassell (clerk); R. Palmer (treasurer); John Greenbank (librarian); and John Kassell (surveyor); together with councillors J. Wilman; J. Taylforth; W. Bayliff (the stonemason who later built the Kirkby Lonsdale Institute); F. B. Punchard; T. Huddart; and G. Duguid. The event ended with 'three hearty cheers' for King George V.

The events following the accession to the throne of King George V came to a climax with his Coronation in 1911. This picture shows the decorated arch (provided as always by the Underley Estate) which was erected to celebrate the occasion, and looks down Main Street towards Town End.

This occasion, marking the Coronation of Her Majesty Queen Elizabeth II on 2 June 1953, may have been the last time the old Underley arch was used. The weather on that day was especially unpleasant with rain and high winds, and the procession was much reduced. Leading it on horseback is Jonty Wilson.

A tree-planting being carried out by Mr E. Clarke at the dedication of Jubilee Field in 1953. The land was given to the people of Kirkby Lonsdale by the Underley Estate with a covenant that it could never be built on. A number of those present can be identified, including Billy Metcalfe, the tall man third from the left. Next to him is Billy Abbott, the agent to the Paget-Tomlinsons and chairman of the council, and in front of him Barbara Hodgson. Jonty Wilson's trilby can be seen peeping up at the back, while at the extreme left are Lottie Howard (in headscarf) with Mrs Davies behind. The two ladies at the front right are Mrs Clarke and Mary Bell (née Smith) who worked in Wolfendens; behind Mrs Bell is Mr Evans the chemist. Mr Barrow Bell is at the extreme right, while between the two ladies is Mr Kennard, the manager of Martins Bank. On Mrs Clarke's right is Councillor Ted Dunn from Biggins. Others present include Margaret and Barbara Wearing, William Fishwick and Maureen Sedgwick. The field remains a popular and much-used recreation area on the banks of the River Lune.

The view down Mitchelgate from the junction with Bective Road is much the same today as in this 1920s picture. Bective Road was constructed in 1895 through a site that was at one time occupied by a chapel (possibly that of the Inghamites). It was so-named in honour of the Earl of Bective. The building carrying the Bective Road sign was originally a 'jerry house' (so-called because men could take their jerrycans there to be filled with ale) called the 'Live and Let Live'. There were several such establishments in Kirkby Lonsdale. Behind the houses on the left (and also the upper houses of Bective Road) were drying grounds where washing could be spread.

Until 1819 the Old Market Cross stood near the junction of Market and Main Streets close to Brantingham's clothes shop. Miss Brantingham had a reputation as a starchy Victorian lady, but according to George Harrison, whenever you bought a pair of trousers or jacket from the shop you would find a 1d or 3d coin in one of the pockets. The Cross now stands at this location in the Swine Market, opposite Abbot's Hall at the junction of Horse Market and Mill Brow. The man wearing the white hat is thought to be William Baines, painter and decorator.

This view of Market Street is reproduced from a postcard sent in March 1917. On the left are the square pillars of the Sun Inn. The lady in the doorway to the left is Mrs Haygarth, the grandmother of Kirkby's local magician, Harry Willan. Three generations of the Willan family were raised in the rooms above the shop (now Foxy Lady) and Harry's father ran the local cinema after the First World War. This was situated opposite on the first floor above what is now the Arcade. On the right, next to the boy pulling the cart, is Sawyer's grocers. The shop sign protruding into the street on the right reads 'Thornborrow, 1d, 3½d, and 6½d Bazaar'. The road ahead leads into Mill Brow and on to Swine Market.

A beck once ran along Market Street and down Mill Brow (right). Except for the stretch between Fountain House and Beck Head it was covered, although there was a trapdoor outside the Sun Inn which could be raised to draw water. Mill Brow could rightly be called the industrial centre of Kirkby Lonsdale, for situated here in the 1800s, on the steep slope down to the River Lune, were bark, bone, corn and saw mills, tanneries and a print works – all water-powered. The smell from these activities must have been quite memorable! This view, probably dating from the 1950s, shows Mill Brow much as it had looked for the previous 100 years. At the foot of the slope was a ford across the River Lune. In order to stop coaches running away as they descended the street, a large square stone was attached to their rear by a chain. One of these so-called 'drag stones' is still to be seen at the corner of Bluebell Cottage in the Swine Market.

In the 1930s there was a bridge at the foot of Mill Brow that crossed to the Island. It was made of concrete blocks with planks between them secured by chains, so that when the river flooded the planks were able to lift off the blocks and hang downstream in the flow. This was the scene of a tragic accident during the Second World War when Marjory, the four year old sister of Jack Sedgwick, crawled off the edge of the bridge and drowned. The structure shown here is somewhat earlier and was situated slightly upstream from the later bridge, crossing to the Island at the shallowest part of the river. Local people can recall it being talked of in the 1900 period. No trace of either bridge can be found today.

This unusual apse-like alcove is built into the high surrounding wall of the back garden of Town End House. The stained glass window carries the letters R. A., for Richard Atkinson, one of two brothers who were benefactors of St Mary's Church. The east window of the church was paid for by Richard Atkinson and dedicated on the Feast of the Annunciation in 1862. It seems likely that this alcove dates from around the same time. The photograph was taken by R. L. Simpson who was active around 1900, and the ladies may be wearing 'widows' weeds', possibly placing the picture around the date of the death of Queen Victoria in 1901. The lady to the right is the wife of the Revd Llewellyn-Davies, while the figure behind the table is unidentified. The other two women are the Murton sisters, Harriet and Eleanor, who once lived in the house. They died in 1931 and 1936 respectively at the ages of 87 and 86, and their grave is marked by a plain rectangular slab adjacent to the Gazebo in St Mary's churchyard.

The stations at Kirkby Lonsdale and Barbon were important points of arrival and departure in the locality, so much so that some of the large houses such as Underley (pages 31–34) constructed their own routes to them. Passenger traffic had ceased by 1962 and the track was removed in 1967. The last stationmaster was a Mr Wetton and the clerk a Claude Brown. The sidings where Harrison's coal merchants kept their stock are to the left in this view. A military parade is shown mustering here immediately before the outbreak of the First World War in the picture on page 27.

Kirkby Lonsdale Bowling Club was founded in 1888 when a quarter acre of land at Tenter Hill (near Harling Bank) was leased from the Earl of Bective for seven years. In 1904 the club merged with the tennis club to form the Kirkby Lonsdale Bowling and Tennis Club. The tennis courts were eventually taken over by Cressbrook School (visible in the background of this picture) and new ones built elsewhere, leaving the bowling club on its original site. At its foundation, the club was a men-only affair and the presence of many women in this picture suggests a social event. Though the date is not known, the photographer R. L. Simpson was active around 1900 and the gentleman with the flowing white beard, Anthony Gibson, saddler, also appears in a picture in Alexander Pearson's *The Doings of a Country Solicitor* taken *c.*1897. This would suggest a date of around the turn of the twentieth century.

Opposite: This photograph was taken at a dance in 1929/30 of the Junior Imperial League (IMPS), the equivalent of today's Young Conservatives. It was held in the concert hall, which also doubled as the local cinema and was situated above the Old Market Hall, now the Arcade at the junction of Market and Main Streets. The men on the balcony are (left) Mr Troughton Snr. and Charlie Pailthorp. Jim Thompson is sitting behind the IMPS poster in the front row with William Fishwick to his right and Ada Richardson, Mary Fishwick and Stan Major to his left. The gentleman with the bow tie in the centre is a Mr Hopewell. To his left is Miss Mansley and to his right Mrs Roper of Casterton Hall. Older readers may also recognise other locals including (towards the back) Harold Bougham, Wilson Dale, Frank Richardson, Billy Dickinson (later killed in a motorcycle accident), Jacky Murray, Jim Jamieson, John Wearing, Norman Hartley, Billy Teasdale, Jim Noble, Ernie Willan, and one of the Hastewell brothers. Closer to the front are Eddie Troughton, Madge Dent, Peggy Clifton, Freddie Tower and Jack Glover.

The Kirkby Lonsdale Company of Westmorland Rifle Volunteers on field training c.1905. At front left is W. E. Fishwick. Such training sessions were a regular part of the activities of the volunteers.

Members of the 1st West Lancashire Field Ambulance, part of the 55th West Lancashire Division, on parade in the coal yard at Kirkby Lonsdale station on 3 August 1914, the day before the declaration of the First World War. From here they were despatched to the Western Front. The name of the station is visible at upper left, and the stone-faced shelter close to the signal appears in photographs taken 30 years later. The photographer, A. G. Price of Hereford, took a series of war photographs at about this time.

The River Lune and local tarns froze frequently between the late 1800s and the mid-twentieth century. This picture from 1926/7 shows a skating party enjoying the ice on Terry Bank Tarn near Old Town. From the left the first three figures are Bill Fishwick, Mrs Tanner and Tony Tanner. The tallest figure on the right is Percy Harrison, with his hands on the young George Harrison's shoulders. Right of Percy in the photograph is Hilda Harrison and left, Mr W. E. Fishwick. Locals may also be able to recognise Agnes Wormwell, Ronnie Dean, Ted Battersby and Ada Holmes. Such cold spells continued until around 1940, which was the last winter that the ice was strong enough for such activities, though some skating was occasionally possible into the 50s and 60s. Great freezes like this were an occasion for fun and festivities, bringing young and old together on the ice.

Below: The approach road to Devil's Bridge reproduced from a postcard sent on 28 July 1930. At the time this bridge was the only dry crossing of the River Lune at Kirkby Lonsdale. The photograph is likely to date from the early 1920s, as the large oak on the left blew down later that decade. Just a few years later, when the new Stanley Bridge was completed, this crossing was closed to vehicles. Devil's Bridge is now a major tourist attraction and one of the most visited places in South Lakeland.

Left: On 29 December 1934, just two years after the closure of Devil's Bridge to traffic, Kirkby Lonsdale experienced a sensational road accident. On a dark night in thick fog, a lorry managed to miss the bend in the road approaching the new Stanley Bridge and went straight on towards Devil's Bridge, finally crashing into the parapet. Its driver could not open his own door which, unknown to him, hung over a drop to the rocks below. Instead he climbed out of the passenger side. He apparently fainted on returning to the scene the next morning and realising how the jammed door had probably saved his life. This picture was presented to the Institute by the then chairman of the council, J. J. Richardson.

About to cut the ribbon to formally open the new Stanley Bridge on 3 December 1932 is the MP for Westmorland, the Hon. Oliver Stanley, after whom it was named. To his right is Lady Henry Cavendish-Bentinck, and to his left G. H. Pattinson (Chairman of Westmorland County Council) and S. H. le Fleming (Lord Lieutenant). Other local people present include Sergeant Robinson, Miss Taylor, Mrs Percy Harrison, William Wolfenden, J. J. Richardson, Mrs 'Pash' Howarth and Miss Madge Alston. The taller of the two boys on the right is a young George Harrison, who claims he rushed forward when the tape was cut to become the first person to cross the bridge following its opening.

Large estates and country houses – notably Underley, Lunefield, Biggins and Rigmaden – played an important role in the historical development of Kirkby Lonsdale and the surrounding area. The Underley Estate was the largest and, at its zenith, reached over 25,000 acres incorporating parts of Dent Dale. Underley Hall was built for Alexander Nowell and completed in 1825. Prior to that, in 1807, Nowell had built Nos. 5 and 7 Fairbank as his temporary residence. No. 5 later became the home of General Wyatt, the man who 'chose' the Unknown Soldier, while No. 7 became the Masonic Rooms when the Earl of Bective was provincial Grand Master. One of the houses opposite the smithy in Fairbank carries on its wall the coat of arms of Nowell (three lidded cups). The estate subsequently became the property of the Cavedish-Bentinck family, and in 1941, following the death of Lady Cavendish-Bentinck two years earlier, Underley Hall was sold and subsequently housed evacuee children from Bournemouth. Following the war it was bought by Oakfield Girls' School. It then became a Roman Catholic Seminary and eventually a special school for children, which it remains to this day.

Underley Hall seen in the distance from what are now the pick-your-own fields in Kearstwick. This apparently idyllic scene, taken in 1942, belies the hardships faced by Britain during the Second World War. Ploughing, as part of the local war-effort quota, are Ted Bainbridge (left) and James Nicholson (right). Though the horses look magnificent, such hand-ploughing required massive physical effort and is no longer practised except in competitions.

A fête in support of the Primrose League taking place on the terrace of Underley Hall around 1905. The Primrose League was a Conservative organisation founded in 1883 and modelled to some extent on the Irish Orange Society, although the branches were called 'habitations' rather than lodges. The League acquired its name because its founder Lord Beaconsfield's favourite flower was the primrose, a wreath of which was sent to his funeral by Queen Victoria. By the early 1900s it had grown into a powerful party organisation. Lord Henry Cavendish-Bentinck was the ruling councillor of the Kendal Habitation of the League at the time of this rally. Judging by the umbrellas it was a wet day!

Underley remained a centre for local events until the start of the Second World War. This picture shows the opening ceremony of a rally and sports day organised by the Kirkby Lonsdale & District Branch of the British Legion on Wednesday 3 July 1929. The ceremony is being performed by Countess Haig, widow of Earl Haig who had died the previous year and who founded the British Legion after the First World War. The gentleman in the foreground is Lord Henry Cavendish-Bentinck, the host for the day. Behind his right elbow is Percy Harrison and to his left, wearing lapel badges, are Billy Abbott (a land agent for several local estates) and George Duguid. The programme, printed by Mrs A. C. Willan (née Haygarth), shows that there were races from 3 p.m. until 6.30, sideshows and an extensive programme of music by the Kirkby Lonsdale Prize Band.

The Cavendish-Bentincks were keen gardeners and had an alpine and heather rockery on the Casterton side of the River Lune. To reach it, estate workers built a catamaran in the late 1800s which could be self-propelled using a hand crank that was connected to cables stretched across the river. Surviving pictures suggest that the boat was rebuilt several times over the following 50 years, and the model shown here appears on a photograph taken c.1935. It states on the reverse that by this time the rockery had become a rose garden. This would be consistent with information that floods in 1927 and 1931 had destroyed much of the original garden, and with the naming of a rose after the Countess of Bective at around the same time. The 'crew' here are sisters Greta and Nan Anderson – whose father was head gardener at Underley – and friends.

An evening's entertainment in the Kearstwick Institute, *c*.1930. This was erected in 1902 by Lord and Lady Henry Cavendish-Bentinck. An inscription on the front wall reads 'For the use and enjoyment of those who lived on the Underley Estate, in memory of Thomas, Lord Bective' (Lady Henry's father). Later, Lady Henry founded and was president of the Kearstwick Women's Institute which, according to *The Annals*, became the first Women's Institute in Westmorland in October 1917, beating that at Levens by six hours! A Grade II listed building, the Institute fell into dilapidation in the 1970s and was used as a game store. It was finally purchased by Ian Radford and his partner and tastefully converted into a family house, winning the Civic Award in 2002. The main characters in this photograph are (from the left) J. J. Richardson (holding bag), Will Pearson, Bob Cantwell and Miles Hastewell (seated), Jonty Wilson (on horse shaking hands) Wilf Hastewell (seated at back of horse) and Mr Jolleys (extreme right).

After being sold to Alfred Harris in 1869, the original Lunefield was demolished and replaced by this building, situated some 50 yards to the north. The Harris family were active benefactors in the Kirkby Lonsdale area for some years, but finally sold Lunefield to the Countess of Bective of Underley in 1899 following the death of the Earl of Bective some six years earlier. The countess, who was the mother of Lady Henry Cavendish-Bentinck, also had a London home, but was prominent in Kirkby Lonsdale in both political circles and the Women's Union. After her death in 1928 Lunefield was purchased by the Co-operative Holiday Association, and, except for a period during the Second World War when it was occupied by the Royal Engineers, remained a holiday home until the late 1950s. Seen here in its heyday c.1905, the second Lunefield was demolished in early 1959 due to dry rot. Both it and its predecessor stood on land now occupied by Ruskin's Drive, Lune Close and Lunefield Drive.

The Biggins, seen here on a postcard sent in 1905, was built in 1895 on a site close to the old Biggins Hall by Dr William Paget-Tomlinson. The Biggins Estate owned many properties in the town and also several farms in the surrounding countryside. Dr Paget-Tomlinson was a great benefactor of Kirkby Lonsdale, making many generous gifts to the church, Institute, grammar school and Clergy Daughters' School in Casterton. He died in 1937, but members of the family still live in Kirkby Lonsdale. During the Second World War The Biggins was occupied by evacuee children from Moorland School, Blackburn, but was destroyed by a fire in 1942 which broke out at a time when all local water supplies were frozen solid. Virtually nothing now remains of it.

Barbon Manor, sited on the fellside at the entrance to Barbondale, is seen here as it appeared c.1912. The house was built in 1863 in French Classical style by Sir James Kay-Shuttleworth to the designs of E. M. Barry. Its tower and west wing were demolished in 1955 but the remainder, remodelled by Claud Phillimore, still belongs to the Shuttleworth family and remains occupied. The Shuttleworths first appeared on the local scene in 1591 when they purchased the Manor of Barbon. The present Lord Shuttleworth lives in neighbouring Leck Hall.

Beckfoot is situated on a lane that loops off the main Kirkby to Sedbergh road a mile beyond Casterton. Part of Barbon Parish, it is no more than a cluster of houses and farm buildings, but features this charming packhorse bridge over Barbon Beck, seen here in the late 1940s. The bridge links Low Beckfoot with High Beckfoot Lane and Treasonfield and was built in 1571, probably by one John Hardy of Barbon at a cost of 22s 4d.

Rigmaden is another country house and estate that has helped shape the landscape around Kirkby. According to Olive Wilson's *A History of Mansergh and Rigmaden*, there are references to it as early as 1206. By 1332 Rigmaden belonged to a Thomas Warde and was eventually sold by Henry Ward in 1660 to Thomas Godsalve, 'a Citizen and Merchant of London and Merchant at Amsterdam'. Godsalve paid £1,700 for Rigmaden Hall and the associated estate. He rebuilt the house, and to this day there remains a carved stone over a blocked arch into the old stable yard carrying a Dutch inscription and the date 1680. After a chequered period in its history, the estate was purchased in 1822 by Christopher Wilson, a Kendal banker who built a new house designed by the well-known local architect George Webster. It has remained in the Wilson family ever since. The estate probably enjoyed its heyday in the early years of the twentieth century when it was occupied by the entrepreneurial Christopher ('Kit') Wyndham Wilson. This picture, taken from an album dated 1904, shows workmen harvesting bark from an oak tree with the house, known as Rigmaden Park, in the background. The bark was used in the tanning industry, though it is doubtful whether any of the Kirkby tanneries were still operating as late as 1904.

Also dating from c.1904, this picture shows Katie (Katherine Edith) Wilson in what was called the 'Tub Cart' or 'Governess Cart' outside the gates of Rigmaden Park. On the gates (which no longer exist) the Wilson coat of arms can be seen. Katie was Kit Wilson's first daughter from his second marriage (to Edith Farquhar), and was born in 1880, dying unmarried in 1926. During this period Kit remained very active in and around the estate. He installed electricity in 1882 – provided by a water turbine, which is still working – constructed the dams that created Kitmere and Wyndhammere, ran a thriving fish hatchery, bred Wilson ponies (a cross between the Hackney pony and the Fell pony and now known as the Hackney pony in Britain but the Wilson pony in the USA), and stocked an extensive deer park in the meadows and woods opposite the house.

Nearly all country houses had a walled garden to provide shelter and a private sanctuary for the family. This was true at Rigmaden where the garden was used to grow vegetables, flowers for the house, and peaches, figs, grapes and tomatoes in the hot houses. This picture is thought to show the head gardener c.1900 with a magnificent display of orchids and ferns.

Rigmaden Bridge, seen here at the beginning of the twentieth century, was built on rocky spurs by Kit Wilson in 1885 to link the estate holdings on both sides of the river and get his carriages to Barbon station. Until then Barrs, Bainsbank and Carradus Fords would have been used. Initially the bridge and lane leading to it were private and had locked gates at each end. The 50 keys in circulation were issued to the family, local people and others including the vicar and the doctor. Public access over the bridge was granted c.1927 during the occupancy of Rigmaden by C. Hulme Wilson. Otter hounds like those in the foreground last met in the Lune Valley as recently as the 1970s. Ironically great efforts are now being made to reintroduce otters, with some success.

By the middle of the twentieth century the estate had undergone a steady decline as a result of death duties, though Rigmaden Farm still prospered. During the war the family welcomed evacuees from schools in Newcastle and Barrow to Rigmaden. This photograph, taken in 1944, shows some of them on the lawn. A handwritten note on the reverse says that these particular children are from Limpsfield Girls' School and Wimbledon Boys' School. After the war serious dry rot was discovered and the threat of the M6 crossing the estate immediately below the house led to its partial demolition. It stood as an empty shell until 1992 when William Wilson, Kit's great-grandson, had the main house rebuilt. This was occupied by his parents, Daphne and Eric Wilson, until the latter's death in 1999. It is now home to his son, William Wilson and his wife Margaret and their daughters.

Two junior evacuees, Brian and Jimmy, at Rigmaden during the Second World War. They are sitting on the conservatory steps on the far side of the house.

Mansergh School was built in 1839 by Christopher Wilson of Rigmaden. He paid £20 a year for the teacher, a practice continued by his sons Edward and William until at least 1880. The last-known head (in the 1920s) was a Miss Margaret Wilson. The school closed some years ago but is still in use as the parish hall. Mansergh was one of several small village schools within the Kirkby Lonsdale district. Others could be found at Casterton, Barbon and Lupton.

Lupton School and the chapel of ease alongside it were built on land made available by the Earl of Bective in 1867. An old tithe barn at Pant End was dismantled as a source of stone and transported to the site by local tenant farmers. Twenty-two children were admitted in 1876, with the roll reaching about 60 by 1898 when the school was enlarged. Electricity was installed in 1949 and the school continued to be used until 1980. The last head teacher was Miss Margaret Wright of Casterton. In this 1926 photograph the apse of All Saints Church can be seen in the background. The children (and their addresses) are:

Eddie Barber (Green Lane End), Alice Parker (Nook), Joe Barrow (Thompson's Fold)
Annie Parker (Nook), May Barrow (Thompson's Fold), Judith Bowness (School Cottage, where her mother lived as caretaker), Edith Stott (Crabtree).

Joe Barrow and Judith Bowness eventually married.

Hutton Roof, which was well-known for its quarries, is just a couple of miles from Lupton. A poster dated *c*.1835 relating to the leasing of Hutton Roof quarries says: 'to be let for a term of years, the Hutton Roof Quarries . . . the respective takers to be declared at the Sun Inn, Kirkby Lonsdale'. This image, probably dating from the late nineteenth century, is one of a pair in which the name of Robert Clarkson can be discerned on a wagon. Clarkson was born in 1836 at Wyresdale, Lancashire but in adulthood was a resident of Carnforth. He is recorded as being a tenant of several Hutton Roof quarries including the Freestone, Old Grindstone and Blue Flag Quarries. He died in 1880. It would appear that the Blue Flag Quarry was taken over from North North (yes – that was his name!) of Whittington Hall and then passed on to J. Clarkson, Robert's son. However, contemporary sources note that 'success never followed the enterprise' and the quarries closed in 1885. The man just left of centre holding the shaft of the wagon has a wooden leg, perhaps the result of a quarrying accident.

The main road from Kirkby Lonsdale to Sedbergh was formerly one of several toll roads in the area. About a mile from Devil's Bridge and shortly before the village of Casterton, the old toll house, seen here c.1910, still stands. The collection of tolls ceased some time in the nineteenth century, but when this photograph was taken the main road was still little more than a sleepy lane.

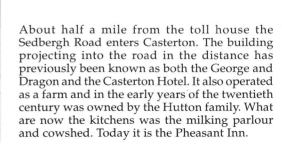

About half a mile from the toll house the Sedbergh Road enters Casterton. The building projecting into the road in the distance has previously been known as both the George and Dragon and the Casterton Hotel. It also operated as a farm and in the early years of the twentieth century was owned by the Hutton family. What are now the kitchens was the milking parlour and cowshed. Today it is the Pheasant Inn.

This picture shows the first Kirkby Lonsdale & District Civic Society committee after its election at the inaugural general meeting on 11 October 1972. The chairman, Col. H. C. W. Bowring is not present but from left to right the other members are: Revd Keith Arnold (who later became the Bishop of Warwick), Jean Leigh, Revd Hugh Rice, Janet Atkins, Hubert Montagu-Pollock (secretary), Dr Graham Mathews and Jimmy Dennison. Cdr. J. D. Gresson was co-opted as treasurer on the first committee meeting on 1 November 1972. Hubert and Graham were made honorary life members in 2002 and still live in the area.